TRUTH TO TELL

This is the second volume in the Osterhaven
lecture series. The M. Eugene Osterhaven
Lectureship was established at Western
Theological Seminary in honor of Professor
Osterhaven at his retirement. Each year
an outstanding theologian addresses
theological themes particularly relevant
to the Reformed faith.

The volumes in the series include:

Wolfhart Pannenberg,
An Introduction to Systematic Theology

Lesslie Newbigin,
Truth to Tell: The Gospel as Public Truth

TRUTH TO TELL

The Gospel as Public Truth

Lesslie Newbigin

William B. Eerdmans Publishing Company
Grand Rapids, Michigan

WCC Publications
Geneva

Copyright © 1991 by Wm. B. Eerdmans Publishing Co.
All rights reserved

First published 1991 in the USA by Wm. B. Eerdmans Publishing Co.
255 Jefferson Ave. S.E., Grand Rapids, Michigan 49503
ISBN 0-8028-0607-4

and in Switzerland by WCC Publications
World Council of Churches
150 route de Ferney, 1211 Geneva 2, Switzerland
ISBN 2-8254-1030-6

Printed in the United States of America

Library of Congress Cataloging-in-Publication Data
Newbigin, Lesslie.
Truth to tell: the gospel and public truth / Lesslie Newbigin.
p.   cm.
ISBN 0-8028-0607-4 (pbk.)
1. Apologetics — 20th cent.   I. Title.
BT1102.N49   1991
239 — dc20   91-21394
CIP

Contents

Introduction

The material in this book was given as the Oster-haven Lectures at Western Theological Seminary, Holland, Michigan, and I must express my gratitude to President Marvin Hoff and Professor George Hunsberger for the honor they did me in inviting me to give these lectures and for the great kindness they showed me during my visit. Several distinguished alumni of the seminary have been my colleagues as missionaries in South India, and I hope that these lectures sustain the missionary commitment which has marked the work of the seminary. For, indeed, these lectures are concerned with the mission of the Church to modernity.

I have used the word "truth" as the key word for the titles of the lectures severally and as a whole because my concern is with the gospel as truth — public truth. This may sound a little like the description a friend gave of the preaching of a well-known Scottish divine: "the defiant proclamation of the obvious." Yet there are at least two reasons for emphasizing this word. The first is that it is widely thought in modern societies that the Christian Church is not so much a source of true knowledge as it is an agency which stands for good values and which is to be supported because it does so. I find it especially important to challenge this view at a time when many churches are responding to the call for a decade of evangelism. I am very glad that this call has been made and is being answered, but I am troubled by the fact that evangelism is — in effect — equated with revival, with a return to values which have been forgotten and need to be reaffirmed. It is not so often acknowledged that evangelism means calling people to believe something which is radically different from what is normally accepted as public truth, and that it calls for a conversion not only of the heart and will but of the mind. A serious commitment to evangelism, to the telling of the story which the Church is sent to tell, means a radical questioning of the reigning assumptions of public life. It is to affirm the gospel not only as an invitation to a private and personal decision but as public truth which ought to be acknowledged as true for the whole of the life of society.

The second reason for emphasizing the word "truth" is that the society in which we have to affirm the gospel is marked by a prevailing skepticism about the possibility of knowing truth. The much-read book *The Closing of the American Mind* by Allan Bloom has evidently touched a nerve in our society. The process which he describes is being carried to its ultimate absurdity in the "deconstruction" program which is extending from literary theory to other branches of what was once thought to be knowledge and which appears to make any claim to speak of truth untenable. In fact, a claim to speak the truth comes to be regarded as only a concealed assertion of power. Nietzsche has come into his own: there is nothing left except the will, since the language of truth is no longer usable.

The book *The Roots of Modern Atheism* by Michael Buckley, S.J., argues that the Church itself must bear heavy responsibility for this situation. In trying to counter skepticism by calling in the help of philosophy to prove the existence of God, rather than by inviting people to believe in God's own revelation of himself in Jesus Christ, the Church abandoned its own proper ground and provided (as Buckley shows) the tools for modern atheism. And, in an even more surprising way, it must be said that the work of missions itself has unwittingly contributed to the relativism of which Bloom complains. Most Anglo-Saxon missionaries were children of the Enlightenment. They did not make the necessary separation in their minds between the Enlightenment's program for human unity on the basis of a universal "reason" with its vision of a single civilization moving progressively toward universality and the gospel program for human unity based in the crucified and risen Jesus. Just as in the Europe of the eighteenth and nineteenth centuries, the confident program of Enlightenment rationalism stimulated a romantic countermovement which extolled the human creativity manifested in the variety of human cultures, so in the nineteenth and twentieth centuries the work of missionaries has been a major factor in stimulating a renaissance of cultures in reaction to the aggression of western rationalism. The modern world has become culturally and religiously plural in a way for which it is unprepared.

The question about criteria becomes urgent. We have learned to acknowledge the cultural conditioning of all claims to know the truth. But if that leads us to abandon as hopeless the search for truth, then our culture is dying. All living creatures must come to terms with a reality beyond themselves which they have to explore and about which they can make mistakes. To abandon hope of speaking truthfully about reality is to abandon the adventure of life. The road that has led us to this point is a long one, but it seems to me that the fatal step was taken when it was supposed that there was available to us a kind of certainty about truth which could excuse us from the duty of taking personal responsibility for our beliefs. It is not only the Christian who is called to walk by faith. I believe that every human being has a responsibility to seek to grasp the truth about the reality which meets us and encompasses us and to state the results of that search, knowing that full comprehension is always beyond us. For the Christian this search is sustained by the promise that, while we now only know in part, a day will come when we shall know as we are known.

In the prevailing climate of subjectivism the affirmation of the gospel as public truth is greeted with skepticism. "What do you mean by 'gospel'? A great variety of religious ideas have been — at sundry times and places — offered under this title. Has not this been so from the beginning? The abstruse metaphysics of the early Church Fathers was something very different from the apocalyptic teaching of the New Testament, and neither is recognizable in the liberal Protestantism of the nineteenth century. All religion, including the Christian religion, is an ever changing affair, and it is futile to appeal to something which lies behind the Christian religion as we now have it — 'the gospel.'" What is to be said in response to this often repeated criticism?

Plainly, Christianity is a constantly changing phenomenon. The gospel, on the other hand, is news about things which have happened. What has happened has happened, and nothing can change it. But, of course, the way we understand what has happened changes. That is why history is always being rewritten — not only because new evidence turns up, but also because old evidence is seen in the light of new experience. The historian E. H. Carr defined history as a continuous conversation between the present and the past. It is only in this way that history becomes part of an intelligible and purposeful life.

If Jesus had written a book, as Muslims believe that the Prophet did, there could not be a real conversation. Jesus, instead, created a human community to which he entrusted the task of interpreting his mission and his message in ever new circumstances. Hence, to the scandal of Muslims, we have four gospels instead of one, and almost all of Jesus' words and deeds come to us in variant versions. Jesus entrusted to his community the responsibility of interpreting all that concerned himself and promised that as his community went out into all the nations, with their varying languages and cultures, they would be led into the fullness of the truth.

In what sense, then, is there an unchanging gospel? In one sense clearly: the story Peter tells on the day of Pentecost, the story he tells in the home of Cornelius, the story Paul tells to the church in Corinth as the one he had originally been told is recognizable as the same story. But yes, of course, it is told in different words on different occasions. All of these tellings of the story claim to be about real events for which there are witnesses, but the way of telling is particular to each situation.

Some contemporary writers are so impressed by the differences that they doubt the veracity of the story. What we call "the gospel," they say, is simply a confused record of a variety of religious experiences. What is accessible to us is not what really happened but the faith of the disciples cast into the form of narrative. My distinction between religions which change and a gospel which does not change is therefore invalid. The inaccessibility to us moderns of "what really happened" is made more certain by two factors: one, the culture of first-century Palestine is so remote from ours that we cannot expect to understand what they were trying to say; and two, it was customary in those days to tell stories to authorize or validate current projects or practices, and everyone understood that these stories were not "history" in the sense that we now understand it.

These last two points are of secondary importance, but it is worth giving a word to each. The argument about cultural remoteness is really a denial of the fundamental unity of the human race. The landless village laborers of South India with whom I have had the privilege of sharing the gospel are at least as culturally remote from me as are the

New Testament writers. Yet they are perfectly able to understand and rejoice in the gospel, although they certainly find their own ways of responding to it. The other allegation about ancient historical (or antihistorical) codes of practice is surely rather absurd. Ancient writers show themselves perfectly capable of distinguishing between fact and fiction. In any case, fiction is useful only in a truth-telling society. If it is understood that alleged facts are normally fictions, fiction loses its usefulness. And finally, the acceptance of this myth would wipe out our claim to know anything reliable about ancient history. Many famous university departments would have to close.

But the main argument is more serious — the argument that what is accessible to us is not what really happened but the faith of the disciples cast into the form of narrative. This view carries weight because it corresponds to a key element in contemporary western culture, namely a false concept of objectivity — of a kind of knowledge from which the human subject has been removed. When it is proposed that a sharp distinction be made between the faith of the first disciples and "what really happened," it is implied that E. H. Carr's continuing conversation should now stop. Of course what we have in the New Testament represents the faith of the disciples, namely their faith about "what really happened." It would be a remarkable example of cultural chauvinism if we supposed that our faith about what really happened, shaped as it is by our own cultural perspectives, must necessarily displace that of the immediate witnesses. The conversation between the present and the past must go on, and will go on, until the end of the world, and the perception of the first witnesses must have the premier role in the conversation.

This line of thinking is obviously applicable to the telling of all history and not only to the telling of the history with which the New Testament deals. Why, then, does it become such a vexing problem when we are dealing with the happenings which form the content of the gospel? We are alerted to the reason by noting that the opening words of the ministry of Jesus include the word *metanoete*. At the very beginning we are warned that to understand what follows will require nothing less than a radical conversion of the mind. I am not competent to embark on a discussion of hermeneutics, but it is obvious that any new fact brought to our attention calls for at least the possibility of a conversion of the mind. Of course, we can only grasp a new fact in terms of the mental resources which we already have. The new fact must be communicated in a language we understand, and we can grasp its significance only by relating it to the vast background of tacit knowledge we have acquired from our nurture since infancy. But the new fact may also be such that it calls for a considerable, perhaps even radical, rearrangement of our mental furniture. We may have, as we say, to change our minds — even in very important ways.

The problem of making sense of the gospel is that it calls for a change of mind which is as radical as is the action of God in becoming man and dying on a cross. With every new fact, or alleged fact, it is always possible — indeed, it is natural — to take note of it without allowing it to change our minds in any radical way. Tacitus could record the fact that someone called "Christus" had been crucified but had given rise to a pestilential sect without this information changing his mind. The two disciples on the way to Emmaus knew that Jesus had been crucified but that had not changed their belief that the Messiah, when he came, would be a successful practitioner of liberation theology. The crucifixion of Jesus was just a ghastly disappointment. What changed their minds, what brought *metanoia*, was the fact that Jesus was alive. And that meant that the crucifixion was a fact of a different kind. As Einstein used to say, what you call a fact depends on the theory you bring to it.

The resurrection is, of course, the point at which the question "What really happened?" becomes most pressing. To believe that the crucified Jesus rose from the dead, left an empty tomb, and regrouped his scattered disciples for their world mission can only be the result of a very radical change of mind indeed. [Without that change of mind, the story is too implausible to be regarded as part of real history. Indeed, the simple truth is that the resurrection cannot be accommodated in any way of understanding the world except one of which it is the starting point.] Some happenings which come to our notice may be simply noted without requiring us to undertake any radical revision of our ideas. The story of the resurrection of the crucified is obviously not of this kind. It may, of course, be dismissed as a fable, as the vast majority of people in our society do. This has nothing to do with the rise of the modern scientific worldview. The fact that a man who has been dead and buried for three days does not rise from the tomb was well known even before the invention of electric lights. If it is true, it has to be the starting point of a wholly new way of understanding the cosmos and the human situation in the cosmos. [In the tradition of the Church the only real analogue for the resurrection of Jesus has been the creation itself. We cannot use any of the tools of science to go behind the creation and ask: "What was there before there was anything?" We can only take the existing world as our starting point.] The resurrection of Jesus from the dead is the beginning of a new creation, the work of that same power by which creation itself exists. We can decline to believe it and take it for granted that we have only the old creation to deal with. Or we can believe it and take it as the starting point for a new way of understanding and dealing with the world. Here two mutually incompatible ways of understanding history meet each other. The "continuing conversation between the present and past" which is the Christian reality in the world is both an ever continuing exegesis of the story which is the gospel and simultaneously a continuing insertion of new creation in the midst of the old.

I am trying to talk about the gospel — good news about something which happened and which, in that sense, does not change. The way of telling it, of understanding it, however, does change. It changes within the time span of the New Testament. But we take leave of serious historical integrity if we replace the record of the first witnesses with myths about various psychological experiences as the origin of the story. There is a gospel to announce today because in the light of the resurrection the whole story of Jesus can be seen not as a series of ghastly misunderstandings and disappointments but as the supreme action of God's holy love, and the whole story of Israel can be seen — as the two disciples on the Emmaus Road began to see it — as having its fulfillment in this action.

And when the Christian Church affirms the gospel as public truth it is not engaged in a self-serving exercise. It is not simply promoting its own growth, though surely the Church rejoices when there are more people who are grasped by the truth as it is in Jesus and are committed to following the true and living way that Jesus is. But when the Church affirms the gospel as public truth it is challenging the whole of society to wake out of the nightmare of subjectivism and relativism, to escape from the captivity of the self turned in upon itself, and to accept the calling which is addressed to every human being to seek, acknowledge, and proclaim the truth. For we are that part of God's creation which he has equipped with the power to know the truth and to speak the praise of the whole creation in response to the truthfulness of the Creator.

Selly Oak   Lesslie Newbigin
March 1991

Believing and Knowing
the Truth

O ne of the three or four books which have been of crucial importance in my own thinking is Charles Cochrane's *Christianity and Classical Culture*, published in 1939. Cochrane, an Oxford classicist, traced the movement of thought from Augustus to Augustine, from the time when classical thought was at the height of its glory to the time when it had disintegrated into nihilism and skepticism and — in the work of Augustine — a new chapter was opened in the story of civilization. Several modern writers, including Michael Polanyi and Alasdair MacIntyre, have drawn parallels between Augustine's time and ours. Classical thought, for all its splendid achievements, had been unable to overcome dichotomies between being and becoming, between reason and will, between the intelligible or spiritual world and the material world

known by the senses. Human history was an un-
ending struggle of virtue against fortune, of the skill
and courage and cunning of the human will against
the blind power of fate which would — in the end
— always prevail. The classical world had lost its
nerve. Truth was ultimately unknowable. In Gib-
bon's tart words, all religions were to the people
equally true, to the philosophers equally false, and
to the government equally useful. And this inward
and spiritual decay was matched by all too visible
disasters until in Augustine's own time the eternal
city, the very citadel of classical civilization, was
captured and sacked by the barbarians.

In the three centuries before Augustine Christian thinkers, deeply versed in the classical culture,
had wrestled to express in its language that which
they had learned from the revelation of God in Jesus
Christ. The result of that wrestling had been crys-
tallized in the Trinitarian formula as articulated at
Nicea and as further developed in the fourth century. Crucial to this formulation was the issue
fought out between Arius and Athanasius. Arius,
backed by the power of the imperial court, would
have adjusted the Christian message to the supposed requirements of contemporary thought. The
old dichotomies could not be denied. The man Jesus
of Nazareth, a figure of flesh and blood accessible
to human investigation, could not be of one substance with God the Father, the eternal spirit in

whom there is no becoming but only being. Athanasius had ranged against him the whole "plausibility structure" of classical culture. It seems almost unbelievable that he should have won the day. The position which we associate with his name, developed and strengthened by later thinking, provided a new model, a new starting point for thought, in fact a new *archē,* as Athanasius said, using the language of classical philosophy. From the point of view of classical thought, as also from the point of view of our post-Enlightenment thought, the Trinity is nonsense. But taken as a fresh starting point for thought, it provided a framework within which the ancient dichotomies were overcome and a new "plausibility structure" was created. There is no more an ultimate dualism of matter and spirit, because God has taken our flesh in such a way that he who has seen Jesus has seen the Father. History is no longer an endless and hopeless struggle of virtue and fortune, of the human spirit against the power of fate, for the one who created and rules all things in heaven and earth, and the one whose Spirit is given to those who are in Christ, is one with the man who went his way from Bethlehem to Calvary, and we can therefore say that God works all things together for good to those who love him.

Augustine was an authentic product of classical culture, trained to its highest level, teacher of rhetoric in the Imperial University. His journey to Christian faith was a long and arduous one, both before and after the critical moment of his conversion. He did not throw away all that he had learned of classical thought as useless baggage, but slowly and painstakingly reassessed it all in the light of the new starting point. He thus made it possible for the western church to carry over into a new culture much of what was good in the old. His lifework illustrates the power which the gospel has shown over and over again to transcend human cultures without destroying them, outlasting them one after another through the centuries and proving its capacity to carry over into new contexts treasures accumulated in older societies.

Augustine is by no means an all-sufficient example of Christian theology at work. The east has never canonized him as the west has done, and there are good reasons for this. Nevertheless I think that Polanyi and MacIntyre are right in suggesting that he has important lessons for us at our moment in the history of the Church, in its long transcultural journey. We are *also* heirs of a culture of extraordinary brilliance. It would be utter folly to try to play down the immense achievements of the past 300 years of western culture. And yet there are many who now try to do this, who are apologetic or even neurotic about its achievements, who engage in masochistic denunciations of western guilt as though the rest of the human race were children who could not be held responsible for their own sins. Western guilt is not ecumenically creative.

But it would also be folly to deny that western culture is in crisis. The perceptive Chinese writer, Carver Yu, looking at our culture from the standpoint of one deeply versed in both Chinese philosophy and Christian theology, sums up what he sees in the phrase: "technological optimism and literary despair." On the one hand he sees the unstoppable dynamism of our technology, always forging ahead with new means to achieve whatever ends — wise or foolish — we may desire. On the other hand he looks at our literature and sees only skepticism, nihilism, and despair. Life has no point. Nothing is sacred. Reverence is an unworthy relic of past times. Everything is a potential target for mockery. There are no honored models to shape behavior. The individual is alone and there are no route maps. Young people ask that question which in a stable society never comes to mind: "Who am I?" And if there is no answer, the simplest way out is to assert the reality of the self by mindless violence, or else submerge the self with drugs.

I think that Polanyi has given us a picture which accurately indicates where we are. The past 300 years, he says, have been the most brilliant in human history, but their brilliance was created by the combustion of a thousand years' deposit of the

Christian tradition in the oxygen of Greek rationalism. Now, he says, the fuel is burned up. We
shall not get fresh light by pumping in more oxygen.
There has to be a renewal of the material on which
critical reason goes to work. Augustine was a rational thinker if ever there was one, but all his great
rational powers could not extricate him from the
disintegrating ruins of classical culture. Reason can
only work with the data that it is given. The new
vision could be developed by Augustine only because there were new data, because through Am-
brose he was brought into living contact with the
Church and with the Scriptures which embody the
story by which the Church lives. Revelation, the
action of God himself in the events which the
Church celebrates, gave him his new starting point.
From a new standpoint his massive intellect could
see in a wholly new perspective the landscape
through which he had traveled. As a result he was
able to hand on to the following centuries a coher-
ent and rational way of understanding the world
and human history which also carried forward
much that was precious in classical culture. But
everything depended on the fact that there was a
new starting point, a new fundamental pattern.
That was given in the Trinitarian faith.

The parallels with our situation are, I think,
instructive. The eighteenth century, the period in
which our modern scientific culture became fully

self-conscious and confident, called itself the Age of Reason. The central conviction which has inspired this brilliant period of human history has been that the human mind is equipped with a power of reason which is capable of discovering the real facts and so liberating us from mere tradition and superstition. But the data upon which reason was set to work were — essentially — the data provided by the senses. Francis Bacon, that pioneer of enlightenment, sought to eliminate all metaphysical concepts and advised us to attend to what he called "facts." To know the facts is to have power over them. The only one of the old metaphysical concepts which he retained was that of cause, because (according to Adorno and Horkheimer) "it alone among the old ideas seemed to offer itself for scientific criticism" (*Dialectic of Enlightenment*, p. 5). The idea of purpose was eliminated as a category of explanation because purpose cannot be directly observed. Bacon's program, vastly developed in subsequent centuries, has given us what Bacon wanted — power, power over nature and, of course, over other people. If we concentrate on "facts" which can be known by the senses, and on causes which can be checked scientifically by observation and experiment, then human reason can obtain power over nature. This has been achieved on an unprecedented scale. The fact that it has alienated us from nature and created a widespread sense of homelessness and bereavement is one of the main reasons for a contemporary rejection of this kind of rationality and the call (in the New Age movement) for a return to the motherly embrace of a Nature that we have so ruthlessly violated. But because human beings are also part of nature, and because the whole driving force of the movement of enlightenment has been to acquire a knowledge of nature which would confer power over nature, the whole thrust of our culture has been toward patterns of domination. Hence the clamorous calls for emancipation of dominated groups which is such a pervasive element in the contemporary scene.

But it is possible for reason to be used in another way. Everything depends upon the data from which reasoning begins. It is possible to begin with the data provided by the five senses and reason inductively from these. This has been the method which has created our modern scientific culture. It still uses the metaphysical category of cause, even though philosophers have questioned it. But it does not use the category of purpose. Purpose is something which is hidden in the mind of the person whose purpose it is until one or other of two things happens. Either the purpose is carried out so that everyone can see what was originally an idea in the mind of the one whose purpose it was, or that person must tell others what his purpose is. There is no third possibility. If we are considering the cosmos as a whole and the human story within the cosmos, and if we are asking whether there is any purpose which would enable us to understand it, the first option is not available. We shall not be around to observe the final moments of the cosmic story. The only available possibility is the second: that the One whose purpose it is should reveal it. If there is no revelation from God, then speech about the purpose of human life can only be specu-lation — the kind of speculation which Bacon ad-vised his contemporaries to avoid in order to study facts.

There was a new starting point for Augustine, as for Athanasius and the Church Fathers before him, because God had acted and spoken in the events which form the substance of the Scriptures, and was still acting and speaking in and through the Church which accepted the Scriptures as God's word. With this, reason had new data to work on. A new possibility opened up for confident and hopeful living even in the darkness of the invading barbarism. The errors of classical thought were rec-ognized and discarded. The positive achievements of classical thought were affirmed and placed in a more secure setting. A vision of the human story was sketched which was vivid and powerful enough to sustain the Church through the horrors of the Dark Ages and to give it the spiritual and intellec-tual resources to bring the barbarian hordes into a new Christian home and to lay the foundations of a new civilization. Everything depends upon the starting point, the *archē*, the assumptions which you take for granted as the basis of your reasoning. It is not (as so often said) a question of reason versus revelation. It is a question of the data upon which reason has to work.

The relevance of this to our situation will be obvious if we recall Carver Yu's characterization of our society: "technological optimism and literary despair." No one can deny the brilliance of our technology. The problem is rather what our technology is used for. We display astounding brilliance in devising means for any end we desire, but we have no rational way of choosing what ends are worth desiring. We develop the technical wizardry of satellite television to bring a cataract of trash into our living rooms. Where do we find the resources for rational decisions not just about means but about ends? I have argued that in this matter reason has no basis to work on unless there is revelation. That is putting it crudely, but I think truly.

Revelation is not allowed as a subject for classroom teaching. It is barred from public doctrine. Human origins are a subject for classroom teaching. They are part of public truth. Human destiny is not. It is a matter of private opinion. And if there is no public doctrine about human destiny, there can be no basis for rational discussion in the public forum about what are and what are not proper ends of human endeavor. And when there are no rational grounds for these decisions, the way is open for the sort of mindless fanaticism about single moral issues which is such a feature of our time. Bacon's vision of unlimited power, and the marvelous achievements of technology which have seemed to authenticate that vision, combined with a purely this-worldly scenario for the human story, and in the absence of any public doctrine about human destiny, creates a situation in which there are no checks on the ruthless pursuit of particular ends, moral or otherwise.

The question of the starting point is the fundamental one. Basic to the shaping of our culture was the attempt of René Descartes to find a fresh starting point for thought. Descartes lived in an age of profound skepticism. It seemed that certain knowledge was impossible. The work of the earlier pioneers of modern science, Copernicus, Galileo, and Kepler, had apparently shattered the world in which the inhabitants of western Europe had felt themselves at home for 1,000 years. It seems that ordinary common sense could not be trusted anymore. The sun does not rise in the east and go down in the west, as it seems to do. It is the earth which is moving even though it feels solid under our feet. Where are we to find certainty in this unstable

world? Descartes, as we know, sought and believed
that he had found a fresh basis for certainty in his
own existence as a thinking mind. From this starting
point he moved to the idea of God — but a God
who is essentially an implicate of the human idea
of perfection, and to the material world which
belongs to a totally different order of existence from
the mind. In this dualistic world God could influence the human mind, but he could not act upon
the material world itself.

Many writers have commented on the way in
which Descartes's dualism has shaped the whole of
our subsequent thinking, creating a dichotomy
which runs right through our culture, a dichotomy
represented on every university campus by the
divide between the science faculty and the faculties
of arts and humanities. At this point I want to draw
attention to a more fundamental flaw in the Cartesian program, a flaw which still affects all our
thinking. Descartes was in search of certitude in an
age profoundly disturbed by the new discoveries.
He lived in a time when beliefs which had been
accepted from time immemorial were being shown
to be unreliable. At all costs it was necessary to find
something which could not be doubted, a foundation on which to build a stable home for the human
spirit. But is it not clear that the whole enterprise
rested on an assumption — an act of faith, if you
like — that the cosmos is so constructed that that

kind of certainty is available to human beings? In that sense Descartes was a child of Christendom. For a thousand years there had been wrought into the very stuff of European thinking the belief that God is to be trusted and that therefore things and people are not simply the playthings of whimsical gods and goddesses or of an all-disposing Fate. Apart from that long schooling, it is hard to think that anyone could have set out on the enterprise to which Descartes set himself. But, and here is the fatal flaw, he sought a basis of certainty in his own mind and not in the faithfulness of God. He opted for a different kind of certitude, not one which trusts in the faithfulness of a gracious God who is not under our control, but a certitude which would very quickly enable Descartes's successors to confront God with the doubt as to whether he really existed at all.

In a sense — I hope not overdramatizing — one could say that the new Cartesian starting point, which has been so foundational for all that has followed, was a small-scale repetition of the Fall. Adam is not content to trust God. He wants to have his own certitude, based on an experimental test of the validity of God's promise. He is the first inductive theologian. We are all Adam's heirs, and we in our particular culture are all heirs of Descartes. This becomes evident when we try to communicate the Christian faith to our unbelieving friends. When we try to do this, the answer comes: "But can you prove it?" "Can you prove to me that Jesus is indeed the true and living way?" "What are the grounds on which I should choose to follow him rather than any of the others who have made similar claims?" We cannot answer that by offering some grounds, something supposedly more reliable than what is given to us in Christ. To do so would be to embark on an infinite regress, since we would in due course have to find proof that these grounds were reliable and then to show further grounds for this and so ad infinitum. What is really being asked, of course, is that we should show that the gospel is in accordance with the reigning plausibility structure of our society, that it accords with the assumptions which we normally do not doubt; and that is exactly what we cannot and must not do. What we have to do is what the Church Fathers and Augustine had to do in the age when classical culture had lost its nerve and was disintegrating. We have to offer a new starting point for thought. That starting point is God's revelation of his being and purpose in those events which form the substance of the Scriptures and which have their center and determining focus in the events concerning Jesus.

Am I propounding the heresy which is called "fideism"? I take this word to refer to the attitude which regards belief as a sufficient substitute for knowledge, which says: "My own belief is good enough for me." This kind of subjectivism is, of course, very widespread in our culture, and is a natural implicate of the loss of belief that truth is knowable. The charge of fideism drives us to the very heart of our problem, which is epistemological. With what right can we claim to know anything? From Descartes onward it has been held that reliable knowledge is to be had by the relentless exercise of the critical method. Dogma can no longer be accepted on its own terms. It must submit to rational criticism. But the critical method must ultimately destroy itself. You cannot criticize a statement of what claims to be the truth except on the basis of some other truth-claim which — at that moment — you accept without criticism. But that truth-claim on which your critique is based must in turn be criticized. The critical principle must ultimately destroy itself. The statement that all dogma must be questioned is itself a dogma which must be questioned. As Polanyi put it, the fuel is eventually all spent. What is left, as Nietzsche saw, is the will to power, that motif which has been at the heart of the program of enlightenment from Bacon onward. Any claim to know the truth is, therefore, simply a concealed assertion of power. And, as Bloom has pointed out, the contemporary language about values is simply a way of concealing the assertion of the will. Values, as distinct from truth-claims — are what somebody wishes. They are a matter of the will. Reason, even the most acutely critical reason, cannot establish truth. And it naturally follows, as a further development of the Nietzschean scenario, that words are treated as nonreferential. They do not communicate truth but assert power. Any claim to know the truth is a claim — well- or ill-disguised — to exercise power.

But the dynamism of our technology is not only an expression of the will to power. It rests on the work of the natural sciences, which have been, at least until recently, inspired by the belief that there is truth "out there" to be explored. Indeed, it would be difficult to understand how knowledge could confer power if it was not knowledge of really existing things. By contrast the other side of our culture, expressed in the literature which Carver Yu had been reading, has largely lost the belief that there is truth to be known — objective realities about which one could say not merely "I think" or "I believe" but "I know."

We can only deal with the charge of fideism by looking at the relation between knowing and believing. We are all heirs of another great Enlightenment figure, John Locke, who defined belief as that upon which we must fall back when knowledge is not available. "Faith," he writes, "is a persuasion of our own minds, short of knowledge" ("A Third Letter on Toleration," quoted by M. Polanyi, *Personal Knowledge,* p. 266). This view of faith is contrasted by Polanyi with Augustine's slogan *Credo ut intelligam,* which Polanyi, as a practicing scientist, sees as a much more true account of the relation between the two. The subjectivism and relativism, the abandonment of belief that there is truth to be known, so trenchantly described by Allan Bloom, is the corollary of a false objectivism which Polanyi has attacked. The originality and power of Polanyi's attack come from the fact that, as a working scientist, he is looking at knowledge from the point of view of the person who is trying to discover the truth rather than from the point of view of the professional philosopher who is dealing with claims to know truth. As a scientist, Polanyi is impressed by all the subjective factors which are involved in the work of scientific investigation. These include social factors: the tradition of scientific work into which young scientists are apprenticed, which establishes guidelines and sets limits, which provides the concepts, methods, and tools with which scientists do their work. And there are the personal elements of intuition, imagination, sound judgment, courage to take risks, and sheer pertinacity without which great scientific work is not done. It is, says Polanyi, absurd to ignore all of this and treat the work of science as though the scientist did not exist, as though the findings of science were simply a transcript of reality, "objective" truth in which the human subject has no place.

Yet it is in this way that the findings of science are often presented to the public in works of popularization or elementary teaching. It is surely obvious that there is no knowing without a knowing subject and that the mind of the subject is involved in knowing.

The effort to know the truth involves struggle, groping, feeling one's way. It is true that there are also moments of sudden illumination, but these come only to those who have accepted the discipline of patient groping, of trying out different possibilities, of sustained reflection. This discipline is one in which we have to begin, of course, as disciples, as pupils. We have to learn a language in which to express what we think we have learned, and the language is itself the form of our knowing. We then go on to struggle with the concepts and models used in the particular field of research until they become part of our minds, and we cease to think about them just as we cease to think about the words we are using. All of this has to be accepted (to begin with) in the faith that those who have gone before us can guide us. We search for clues and, if they are to be useful, we have to believe in them — at least provisionally. Personal commitment in faith and personal judgment about evidence are required at every stage. There is no absolute separation of faith and knowledge. We believe in order to understand. And at every stage we may be wrong. There is no guarantee against error. All our knowing is a personal commitment in which we have no external guarantee that we cannot be mistaken. But we only grow in knowing as we take risks and accept responsibility. Descartes's program of indubitable knowledge is a fatal blind alley. All knowing is the knowing of a fallible human subject who may be wrong but who can only know more by personally committing himself to what he already knows. All knowing is a personal commitment.

Does that mean, then, that knowing is purely subjective? No! It is a matter of personal commitment, but commitment to the understanding of a reality which is not in my mind but "out there." And the proof of this is in my willingness to publish it and to test it in all relevant situations. The alternative to subjectivity is not an illusory claim to objectivity, but the willingness to publish and to test. And this has obvious relevance to the Christian claim that Jesus is the true and living way, the master clue by following whom we shall be led into the truth. We do not validate this claim by calling to our aid some philosophical system based on other grounds. There are no more reliable grounds than what are given to us in God's revelation. The proper answer to the charge of subjectivity is world mission, but it is world mission not as proselytism but as exegesis. Let me try to spell out what I mean.

The Church lives by the faith that (to put it in

a very truncated form) Jesus is Lord. That means that he is Lord not only of the Church but of the world, not only in the religious life but in all life, not merely over some peoples but over all peoples. He is not just my savior, but the savior of the world. We have no way in which we can demonstrate the truth of that claim by reference to some supposedly more ultimate realities. If it is true, it is true for all and must not be concealed from any. But we cannot yet know what its truth means until the Lordship of Jesus has been manifested in the lives of all peoples and in all sectors of human living.

This means that we are engaged in a two-way exercise. We have a story to tell, a name to communicate. There are no substitutes for this story and this name. We have to name the name and tell the story. But we do not yet know all that it means to say that Jesus is Lord. We will have to learn as we go along, as Peter had to learn from his encounter in the household of Cornelius. We are missionaries, but we are also learners, only beginners. We do not have all the truth, but we know the way along which truth is to be sought and found. We have to call all people to come this way with us, for we shall not know the full glory of Jesus until the day when every tongue shall confess him. And we do not know the fullness of what the service of Jesus means until we have struggled to bring all the manifold works of learning and industry and politics and the arts into obedience to him. So mission is not a one-way promotion but a two-way encounter in which we learn more of what the gospel means. We are learning as we go. That is the only way we affirm that the gospel is not just "true for us" but true for all. The missionary action of the Church is the exegesis of the gospel.

What I am saying may sound like familiar missionary rhetoric, but I am saying it in the context of our missionary obedience here in this western culture by which we have been formed and in which we have our being. We cannot demonstrate the truth of Christianity by reference to something else. We have to abandon the idea that there is available to us or to any other human beings the sort of certitude that Descartes wanted to provide and that the scientific part of our culture has sometimes claimed to offer. We have to thank the scientists for keeping alive at least in one part of our culture the belief that there is truth to be known. We also have to thank scientists in more recent times, like Polanyi, for their recognition of the fact that all knowing involves the commitment of the fallible human subject. The tragic legacy of Descartes's proposal has been that the other half of our culture, the half into which theology usually falls, has lapsed into subjectivism. The shadow cast upon the other half of our culture by the massive creations of a

supposedly "objective" natural science has robbed
the liberal arts of the confidence that they also are
avenues along which truth may really be grasped.
So everything becomes subjective.

The false dichotomy is set up between "I
know" and "I believe." Everything in theology becomes subjective. What we call Christianity is one
of the many varieties of religious experience, and
its truth-claims are set aside on the ground that they
arise out of particular cultural contexts. All this
nonsense bears witness to that shadow of which I
spoke, the shadow cast by the idea that there is
available, or should be available, a kind of knowledge which is not the knowledge of a fallible human
subject living in a specific cultural context but is,
to use the blessed word again, "objective." That
idea is simply illusion, and it has become so powerful that it can rob the Christian of the freedom to
say simply: "I know whom I have believed." If one
may continue to use this kind of language, the great
objective reality is God but he is also the supreme
subject who wills to make himself known to us not
by a power that would cancel out our subjectivity,
but by a grace that calls forth and empowers our
subjective faculties, our power to grow in knowledge through believing. We believe in order to understand, and our struggle to understand is a response to grace. Real understanding becomes
possible not by seeking a certitude apart from grace,

but by accepting the calling to seek understanding while knowing that full understanding will be a gift of grace beyond the horizon of our own searching.

I began this chapter by drawing a parallel between our situation and that of Augustine living amid the disintegration of the Graeco-Roman classical culture. I suggested that the important thing was the acceptance of a new starting point. The new vision for human life on this planet did not derive from any abstract idea or first principle. It derived from the revelation of God in Jesus Christ. The *logos,* by which and for which all things exist, had become flesh, part of human history, accessible to human knowledge. Because of this, it was possible to see all things in a different perspective. The stubborn dichotomies are overcome. The power that controls all the visible world, and the power at work in the human soul, is one with the man who went his way from Bethlehem to Calvary. But the Trinitarian model cannot be founded upon any supposedly more ultimate principles. God's revelation in Jesus Christ is the starting point.

I find that when I make this affirmation among my liberal Christian friends it causes anger. It threatens what have been accepted as axioms — namely the right and power of the human mind to make its own decisions about what is true. It appears as a threat to the basis of our free societies. It threatens the efforts to bring unity into a pluralist culture. It threatens the great achievements of the past 300 years which have brought into existence the world we know. It is reactionary. It is fundamentalist.

I can sympathize with this anger and fear. I want in the next chapter to try to address it. But I close now with a reference again to my starting point. Let me put my point negatively. If there had been no Christian Church, classical society would still have disintegrated. The barbarians would still have invaded the Roman world and sacked the imperial city. Everything that the classical world had achieved could have been swept away in the flood. The fact that it was not, that much of its most precious achievement was preserved and made available in later generations to the descendants of those barbarians, was because the great Christian thinkers of the first four centuries had developed new patterns of thought which could safeguard what was most precious in the classical tradition, and — beyond them — because ordinary Christians were willing to die for the claim that Jesus, not the Roman Emperor, is Lord. The Catholic Church was that new society, based on a new foundation, which could hold in trust the real treasures of classical culture even while it denied the foundation on which that culture had been built. To those who fear that a fresh and unambiguous affirmation that the gospel of Jesus Christ must be the starting point and the criterion of all human thought and action will threaten the achievements of the Enlightenment and of those who have shaped our society on its principles, we can say with confidence that, on the contrary, we are offering the only basis on which the true fruits of the last 300 years can be saved from the new barbarians. But to say that is to set a daunting agenda for the universal Church today — no less than to show in both public and private life what it means to confess Jesus as Lord.

Affirming the Truth in the Church

I spoke of the anger which one often meets among liberal Christian friends when the point is made that the starting point for true thinking and speaking about the world and the human situation, its meaning and purpose, must be God's revelation in Jesus Christ. And I gave reasons for some sympathy with this anger, for when the claim is really understood it undermines the most fundamental dogma of our contemporary society. I said that it often led to the charge that the speaker is a fundamentalist — if not openly, at least in his heart. The words "liberal" and "fundamentalist" are freely used among us as terms of abuse and contempt. In this mutual hostility, which is so damaging to the Church's witness, we are in danger of evading the real issues on which the gospel must challenge our culture. It is obvious that this damaging split in the

— 41 —

life of the Church is only one manifestation of the much deeper split which runs through the whole of our culture. I referred to it in the first chapter as the split which is visible on every university campus between the faculties of science and of the arts. It is the split created by a false ideal of objectivity which has the effect of devaluing all kinds of knowing which are not amenable to demonstration by the methods of natural science. I gave reasons for thinking that all knowledge has of necessity two poles, the knowing subject on the one hand and the reality "out there" which that subject is seeking to know. What has happened is a falling apart of these two poles, and I have suggested that the healing of this split can be achieved by considering knowledge from the point of view of the discoverer, the researcher, the explorer, rather than from the point of view of the philosopher who is dealing only with asserted claims to knowledge.

This split has deeply infected the Christian community. On the one hand there are those who seek to present the Bible as a body of objective truths in which human subjectivity plays no part. Consequently there is a tendency to play down all those elements of human subjectivity and fallibility which are involved at every stage — from the very first words written or spoken, through many many stages of recording, revising, editing, selection, translation, printing, and publishing until the book is actually in my hands. But this is to deny the true character of the Scriptures. At every stage in this process we are dealing with fallible human beings whom God is calling to listen, understand, and follow. We read the Bible as ourselves part of the continuing community for which the Bible is the clue to the meaning of the whole human story. We read it as fallible human beings. We read it not as individuals but as part of the people whose story it is. In the reading of it we are brought into the presence of the one who is the true author of the story, the living God who called Israel out of Egypt and who called his beloved Son out of the grave. We are summoned to the same adventure of faith as that of those whose story the Bible tells.

On the other hand there are those who are known, and sometimes abused, as "liberals." Here we have the opposite danger. Everything is human subjectivity. The key word is "experience." We are not dealing directly with the acts and words of God, but with human religious experience which has interpreted events in a religious way on the basis of their cultural traditions and assumptions. The Bible is understood as a record of human religious experience. As such it can hardly claim uniqueness but must be put alongside other literature, both sacred and secular, which testifies to similar experiences of what one may call the religious dimension of human life. And we must agree that *of course* the Bible is a record of human experiences. And these experiences are *of course* the experiences of people who belonged to a particular culture and used the language and thought-forms of that culture. What other kind of human experience could there be? There is an odd innocence about much of the language which is used in this connection, as though there were accessible to us some kind of knowledge which is not the knowledge of people shaped by a particular culture, as though the critic were standing on a supracultural platform. It is once again the illusion of an impossible objectivity. The great work of liberal scholars over the past two or three centuries in disentangling the various strands which have been woven together to form our Bible, and in identifying the particular cultural, political, social, and economic contexts in which they were shaped, has indeed been of value. But, once again, the critical principle, if absolutized and taken as the supreme guide, necessarily destroys itself. Every possible finding of critical scholarship is itself open to criticism. The question is, "On the basis of what assumptions does the criticism rest?" Too frequently it must be said that it rests on the assumptions which are currently unquestioned in the particular society of which the scholar is a part. The criticism, like everything human, is culturally conditioned. When we use the word "experience" we must surely always ask: "Experience of what?" We cannot rest on the subjective pole alone. We have to ask, in full personal responsibility for the answer: "What is the reality of which that experience was evidence?"

If I may refer again to Polanyi, his great task, which he saw as a necessary service both to science and to society as a whole, was to heal the split between the objective and the subjective poles of our knowing. One of his central theses was that all knowing has what he called a "from–to" structure. We grasp an object by turning our attention *from* a multitude of subsidiary clues *to* the meaning of the whole. An obvious example is our reading of a text. We do not focus our attention on the letters which make up the words. We focus our attention on the meaning of whole sentences and we are only aware of the words in a subsidiary way. We shift our focus *from* the letters and words *to* the meaning. Sometimes the subsidiary element is below the level of consciousness — as, for instance, the functioning of the physical components of the eye. Sometimes we can attend to them as we can focus our attention on a particular word, or on the particular sensation in our fingertips when we are feeling our way in the dark. But we only give focal attention to these in order that we may return to focus attention on the meaning of the whole sentence, or on the shape of the thing we are feeling. We turn *from* the subsidiary clues *to* the reality "out there" which we are exploring.

In Polanyi's language, we *indwell* the clues. We

do not look *at* them, but from them to the object of our attention. When we explore a hidden object in the dark with the tips of our fingers, we indwell our fingers. They are part of us, and we are in them. But this is the way we indwell our tools and the many instruments we use. I do not look at my eyes but indwell them, and so also with the lenses of my spectacles. When I talk I do not look at my language as an outsider; I indwell it. It is part of me, and it is the means through which I try to understand the world. And clearly one can extend this concept to the whole of our culture, to all the ways of handling complicated ideas, of conceptualizing complex operations which we use every day. We do not attend *to* the words and concepts, unless it is clear that they are letting us down and that we need new words or concepts. We indwell them. We turn our attention *from* them *to* the matter in hand.

I want to suggest that this Polanyi model can help us in dealing with the sad quarrel between our objectivist fundamentalists and our subjectivist liberals. When a reviewer of my book *Foolishness to the Greeks* said that to pretend that the Bible could provide a basis for a critique of our culture was as absurd as pretending to move a bus when you are sitting in it, he was looking *at* the Bible but he was indwelling our post-Enlightenment culture. He was sitting in the bus. He obviously feels that it is not letting him down. He intends to remain in the bus, seat belt fastened. But it is also possible to indwell the Bible story so that you do not so much look *at* the Bible from without as look at the world from within the Bible, through the lenses that the Bible gives you. As one Latin American theologian has said, the business is not so much to understand the text as to understand the world through the text. Of course the first cannot be neglected. Before you can use a language in such a way that you are not thinking about the words but about the meaning you want to convey, you have first to learn the language. You have to attend focally to the words before you can get to the point at which you focus on the meaning and only attend in a subsidiary way to the words. You turn *from* the words *to* the meaning. I am suggesting therefore (and I think this is in line with what George Lindbeck has suggested) that our use of the Bible is analogous to our use of language. We indwell it rather than looking at it from outside.

But for this to happen it is clear that this "indwelling" must mean being part of the community whose life is shaped by the story which the Bible tells. When we live as part of this story, constantly remembering and reenacting its crucial events, as we do in the liturgy of the Church, it becomes like our language. It provides the models and concepts through which we seek to understand and cope with the events of daily life. In a stable

Christian community we learn it in the same way
as we learn our mother tongue. And since the
understanding of the whole human story which
permeates the Bible is radically different from that
which permeates our contemporary public life,
there are clearly the preconditions for an encounter
with our society. We are not obliged to sit in the
bus with seat belts fastened. There is another possibility. But, plainly, the encounter is not between a
book and our culture. The parties in the encounter
are in both cases living communities of people. The
Bible is a disembodied language like Esperanto, if
it is detached from the continuing life of the community that speaks this language. When, on the
other hand, it is the living language of a living
community, its reliability will be shown not by
validating it against some external criteria, but by
the way in which it enables the community that
uses it to make sense of the whole complex world
of things and happenings which human beings
have to face — and by "making sense" I mean both
understanding and coping with. To put it very
shortly, our faith is that this is the language which
does make sense because the word of God, made
flesh in Jesus, is that by which and for which all
things were made. In other words, this language is
not just our particular vernacular. When we learn
it and begin to speak it fluently, we discover that
it has one great advantage: it is the language of

government — that government which is supreme over all the usurpers.

Our problem is that most of us who are Christians have been brought up bilingual. For most of our early lives, through the accepted systems of public education, we have been trained to use a language which claims to make sense of the world without the hypothesis of God. For an hour or two a week we use the other language, the language of the Bible. We are like the Christian congregations under the *milet* systems of the Persian and Muslim empires: we use the mother tongue of the Church on Sundays, but for the rest of our lives we use the language imposed by the occupying power. But if we are true to the language of the Church and the Bible, we know that this is not good enough. The incarnate Word is Lord of all, not just of the Church. There are not two worlds, one sacred and the other secular. There are differing ways of understanding the one world and a choice has to be made about which is the right way, the way that corresponds to reality, to the reality beyond all the show which the ruler of this world can put on. It is not a question of the Church versus the secular world. The boundary between two realms runs through each of us. We all, I am sure, whether we are labeled as liberals or as fundamentalists, struggle and groan inwardly as we try to relate what we do and say and sing on Sunday with what goes on in the rest of the week. We are indeed, as the title of a recent book reminds us, "resident aliens." But we are not a *milet* existing by courtesy of the dominant power. Nor are we merely an expatriate community preserving the style of the folks back home with a compound wall to keep out the natives. We are here as missionaries because the one whom we serve is rightful Lord of all.

It is very tragic that in this missionary task which calls for all our spiritual resources, we should be so deeply divided among ourselves. For Protestants at least, in the present situation, the crucial question is the authority of Scripture as it is acknowledged and exercised in the life of the Christian community. I have suggested that this question cannot be dealt with except by means of a radical critique of the reigning epistemology, the way in which we regard any claim to know the truth. On the one side there are those who claim for the Bible a kind of authority which it cannot have, an authority which would obliterate the subjective factors which are involved in human knowing of anything. On the other side are those for whom the Bible has no real authority at all because it is simply one strand of the many-stranded fabric of human religious experience. Both parties are led astray by Descartes's dream, by the false ideal of an indubitable knowledge. I think it is almost impossible to exaggerate the influence which this dream has had.

It appears constantly in the arena of interfaith discussion — the idea that there is or could be available to us a stance from which we could survey and evaluate the world's religions, identifying the good and the bad elements in each from a standpoint which was neutral, impartial, raised above the particularity of any. It appears in the attempt of Christian apologists to demonstrate the truth of Christianity on the basis of supposedly self-evident truths. Above all it appears in the pervading relativism which abandons as hopeless the quest for knowledge of the truth outside a limited area of empirical facts, and leaves people, especially young people, to wander without a clue.

Polanyi's effort to reform the epistemological basis of science was directed against objectivism, against the illusion that we can evade personal responsibility for our assertions of truth. He insisted on the fact that all knowing involves the personal participation of the knower, that it always involves the risk of being wrong, and that the struggle to know, to understand, to comprehend, calls for the fullest exercise of personal responsibility.

> Comprehension is neither an arbitrary act nor a passive experience, but a responsible act claiming universal validity. Such knowledge is indeed *objective* in the sense of establishing contact with a hidden reality; a contact that can be

defined as the condition for establishing an indeterminate range of yet unknown (and perhaps yet inconceivable) true implications. (M. Polanyi, *Personal Knowledge,* pp. vii-viii)

There is no knowing without the willingness to search, to explore, to take risks. "Only affirmations which could be false," he says, "can be said to convey objective knowledge of this kind" — that is to say, knowledge which proves to be objective by the fact that it leads on to further knowledge. The ideal of a kind of objectivity which eliminates personal responsibility is false and deceptive.

Polanyi was writing as a scientist, concerned to rescue science from what he saw as a false track. But, as has been widely recognized, his epistemology has larger implications, including — I suggest — implications for the Church. Perhaps these are especially important at a time when many in the churches are calling for a decade of evangelism. There can be no true evangelism except that which announces what is not only good news but true news. It is a very serious matter when the gospel is marketed primarily as a panacea for personal or public ills. We believe that it is indeed for the healing of the nations, but it cannot be this if it is not true. How can we affirm the gospel as true in a pluralist society where all such claims are bracketed out of public life and relegated to the area of private opinion? The very fact that its truth can be doubted, and is in fact doubted by a majority of human beings, is regarded as sufficient to exclude it from public doctrine. Public doctrine, as currently understood, has to deal with "facts" which are objectively true and not matters of personal opinion. (Of course the fact that people hold different opinions is a fact which can be recognized as part of public truth. There can be courses in comparative religion or in comparative political theory. But care has to be taken to ensure that the teaching is impartial and objective.) Objectivity is taken to mean freedom from risk. But, in truth, all knowing involves the possibility of being mistaken. Of course these risks have to be responsibly taken. As Polanyi says, comprehension is not an arbitrary act. It requires us to take with the greatest seriousness the findings of past generations, using them as the base for further exploration. The Church must always understand itself to be on pilgrimage, *in via*. It takes the tradition with which it is entrusted as the guide for the exploration of new realities, and the exploration of new realities in turn modifies and emends the tradition. The tradition is trusted to embody true understanding. It provides the framework by means of which we can grasp and place new experience. In that sense we *dwell in it* a-critically. But that does not mean that it is infallible or incorrigible. We do not guard it as a precious antiquity. We affirm our belief in its truth by the boldness with which we continue to explore new realities by its aid, with the confidence that it gives, in the light that it sheds.

From a Polanyian perspective both objectivism and subjectivism are simply evasions of responsibility. In both cases one proposes to avoid risk. And that criticism applies to the particular manifestations of these two errors which are fundamentalism and liberalism. In his recent book *Unapologetic Theology* Dr. Placher quotes with approval Mac-Intyre's definition of tradition as "a historically extended, socially embodied conversation," and he summons Christians to be active in this conversation. This involves taking the risks that serious conversation involves, and it is in line with what I am trying to suggest. I am trying to suggest a way forward which is not that of either the fundamentalist or the liberal. If one may risk unfair caricature, the danger in the first case is that the colony of resident aliens becomes a ghetto. The danger in the second case is that it loses its sense of a specific mission. Serious exploration is replaced by aimless wandering, by jumping onto every passing bandwagon to see whether it might lead to somewhere interesting. In the blessed name of "relevance" the thrust of the gospel is lost in a series of alliances with enthusiasms each of which is quickly discarded in favor of another. By speaking of knowledge as personal, Polanyi wanted to describe a way which escapes both objectivism and subjectivism. It is a way which emphasizes the essential role of tradition and the relationship of personal commitment to potentially hazardous developments of the tradition. The central emphasis is on personal responsibility in the search for a true comprehension of reality.

The split between a bogus objectivism and the resultant collapse into subjectivism is reflected in the discussions which take place in the political field. The recent collapse of the communist regimes in eastern Europe has fueled a mood of euphoria in the western world about the all-sufficient benefits of a free society. Pluralism is contrasted with totalitarianism as light with darkness. Yet we in our society know much and are learning more about the problems of pluralism. Total pluralism, in which there are no criteria by which different life-styles could be evaluated, in which any kind of discrimination between cultural norms as better or worse is forbidden, in which there is no truth but only "what seems meaningful for me," leads inevitably to anomie, to lostness, to a meaningless life in a meaningless world. Marxism claimed to be a scientific account of human affairs, objectively true apart from any value judgments or moral passions. As such it claimed the right to impose itself as public doctrine controlling all aspects of life. Although Marxism had a powerful appeal to moral passions for justice and equity, it claimed to be true entirely without reference to the moral passions which it despised. It was just objective truth and therefore historical necessity. We have seen the disastrous consequences of this doctrine which has cast its shadow over the intellectual as well as the political life of the world for most of this century, and we have applauded the collapse of the regimes which were founded on this doctrine. In this situation pluralism has become the word by which we designate the kind of society we want to live in. A free society is a pluralist society. From the disastrous consequences of a false objectivism, we are in danger of collapsing into a false subjectivism where there are no criteria but everything goes.

I would like to suggest that we distinguish between two kinds of pluralism. I would like to label them "Agnostic Pluralism" and "Committed Pluralism." By the former I mean, of course, the kind of pluralism in which truth is regarded as unknowable, in which there are no criteria for judging different kinds of belief and behavior. It is the kind of pluralism which increasingly operates in what are called the "free" societies. In using the term "Committed Pluralism" I am following Polanyi in his vision of knowledge as neither purely objective nor purely subjective but as that which is available to the person who is personally and re-

sponsibly committed to seeking the truth and pub-
licly stating his findings.

The background for this is, of course, Polanyi's
own experience of what he used to call "the republic
of science." The scientific community is pluralist in
the sense that it is not controlled or directed from
one center. Scientists are free to pursue their own
lines of investigation and research. They are free to
differ from one another and to argue with one
another, and they do. But they operate within a
tradition which embodies the findings of past members of the republic. The tradition is not infallible
or incorrigible. On the contrary it is constantly
being modified by new discoveries. But it nevertheless provides a firm framework for scientific research. No one becomes a member of the republic
who has not successfully completed a long appren-
ticeship to the tradition under the direction of those
who are its acknowledged masters. There is freedom, but not anarchy. There are norms which have
to be respected if research is not to become futile.
Long-established views are not cast aside without
a very great deal of experimental work, and — in
any case — not until a more viable theory has become available. Freedom of thought and speculation is limited by what has already been well established as truth. And because it is believed that there
is reality about which the truth may be — if only
partially and provisionally — known, the findings

of scientists are published for critical examination and testing by others. And, once again, because it is believed that there is reality to be known, differences of opinion are not left to coexist side by side as evidence of the glories of pluralism. They are the subject of debate, argument, testing, and fresh research until either one view prevails over the other as more true, or else some fresh way of seeing things enables the two views to be reconciled as two ways of seeing one reality.

The scientific part of our culture is by far the most dynamic part. Granted the difference between the data with which the natural sciences deal and those with which students in other disciplines deal, I am compelled to ask whether these justify the huge gap which exists between these two parts of our culture in respect of our search for the truth about reality, and whether the republic of science does not offer a model for a kind of pluralism which is not agnostic and anarchic, but committed and responsible in the search for the truth. Perhaps the slogan "A Responsible Society," which was current in the World Council of Churches forty years ago and which was coined in the debate between communism and laissez-faire capitalism, has a wider application. What might this mean in practice?

It would mean, in the first place, that just as we refuse to believe that there is no third possibility between a false objectivity and a false subjectivity, both of which have as their common factor the abdication of personal responsibility to seek out and know the truth, so in the public field we refuse to accept the idea that there is no third possibility between some sort of theocracy, perhaps a return to an idealized picture of medieval Christendom, on the one hand, and agnostic pluralism on the other. The corollary of Polanyi's idea of responsible personal knowledge is a society in which this responsibility is acknowledged and respected. Clearly the Christian Church ought to be the model and the nursery of such a society. It can be so only if we can extricate ourselves from the false dichotomy of objective and subjective, which is reflected in the battle between liberals and fundamentalists, and the key lies in the acceptance of personal responsibility for seeking to know the truth and for publishing what we know. Both objectivism and subjectivism are ways of evading personal responsibility for knowing the truth. That seems to me to be the crucial point. And if this is so, then the call to the Church is to enter vigorously into the struggle for truth in the public domain. We cannot look for the security which would be ours in a restored Christendom. Nor can we continue to accept the security which is offered in an agnostic pluralism where we are free to have our own opinions provided we agree that they are only personal opinions. We are called, I think, to bring our faith into the public arena, to publish it, to put it at risk in the encounter with other faiths and ideologies in open debate and argument, and in the risky business of discovering what Christian obedience means in radically new circumstances and in radically different human cultures.

In a society where agnostic pluralism reigns, freedom is understood to be the liberty to do what you want provided it does not interfere with the freedom of other people. Freedom is the absence of limits. In that case, the ideal model of freedom would be an astronaut, floating weightless in space and out of contact with the spacecraft. Obviously such a man would not be free at all, for freedom means the possibility of choosing between options in the real world, and the more we learn about the real world the less scope there is for fantasy. A society in which any kind of nonsense is acceptable is not a free society. An agnostic pluralism has no defense against nonsense. So while a committed pluralism values freedom as the necessary (though not sufficient) condition for grasping the truth about the real world, the fundamental relation between truth and freedom is that enunciated by Jesus when he said, "The truth shall make you free." That saying, we remember, provoked the furious anger of the hearers, who affirmed that they were free already and did not need anyone to set them free. Jesus tells them that they are not free until the truth makes them free, and they respond by threatening to stone him. When we affirm, as the Church must do, that freedom is not the natural endowment of every human being but is something to be won by acknowledgment of the truth, and that in the end the truth is something given in the sheer grace of God to be received in faith, there is bound to be anger. There is bound to be the feeling that the free society is once again threatened by dogma. I think the Church cannot evade the sharpness of this encounter.

Christians are not, of course, the only ones who are questioning the whole foundation of our culture. The popularity of the New Age movement is very understandable. There is a justified recognition of the fact that the whole movement of enlightenment, from Bacon onward, has been concerned with power, the power which knowledge gives us over nature, and also, eventually, over other people. The movement initiated by Bacon, leading as it has done to the vast development of science and of technology based on science, has given us a mastery over nature which has alienated us from nature. There is a deep feeling of bereavement, of the loss of our original unity with the natural world. Those whom we used to call primitive peoples, those who have escaped our civilization and therefore escaped our alienation and bereavement, now seem to us examples of how we ought to live. We have over-developed one half of our brains, and we need to recover what we have lost, the capacity to see things whole, not seeking to master everything by dissection, analysis, and the experimental methods that force nature to answer the questions we put to her, but accepting and rejoicing in the wholeness of things. We cannot deny the large elements of truth in this protest. And most certainly the global ecological crisis which now confronts us must require a radical rethinking of the course we have taken in the past 300 years in manipulating and exploiting nature for our self-chosen purposes. We surely do need another kind of rationality than the one which is so brilliant in devising means but so helpless when it comes to discerning ultimate ends.

The New Age movement, for all the validity of its protest and the value of some of its recommendations, is in truth a very old blind alley. There is a very long history to remind us of what happens when nature is our ultimate point of reference, from the Ba'al worshippers of the Old Testament to the worshippers of blood and soil in Nazi Germany. Nature knows no ethics. There is no right and wrong in nature; the controlling realities are power and fertility. Nature sometimes has a charming smile, but her teeth are terrible. And, moreover, modern science tells us that there is one law of nature which no scientist will question, the so-called Second Law of Thermodynamics, which tells us that

every closed system necessarily runs down into ran-
domness. The sun pours forth its energy, and nothing will restore it. All things decay. If, therefore, the
whole of nature, the cosmos, is to be understood
as a closed system fully explicable without reference
to anything beyond it, then there is no escape from
this conclusion. As a modern scientist has recently
put it, the deep structure of change is decay. If
nature has the last word, then that is it.

Our faith is that the cosmos is not a closed
system and that the Second Law does not have the
last word; that the cosmos is created by the word
of God, and that that word is continually active in
the whole of the cosmos to renew and to create out
of decay new patterns of order, to raise the body of
Jesus from death to a new creation in glory, to
renew the face of the earth and to renew the whole
life of humanity. If nature has the last word, that
word is death. But if it is true that the last word,
as also the first word, is that which was in the
beginning, has become part of our history in the
man Jesus, and will be manifest at the end as the
consummation of all human and cosmic history,
then we cannot accept the call, seductive as it is, to
sink back into the embrace of mother nature. Nor
can we accept a kind of pluralism which confuses
the normal with the normative, which supposes that
the unity of humankind can be achieved by raising
no question of ultimate truth, a false and deceptive

ecumenism which advocates unity as an end in itself and denies the central claim of the gospel, that it is Jesus, the crucified and risen Jesus, who is alone the center around which alienated human beings can be drawn together in a reconciled fellowship.

We have a gospel to proclaim. We have to proclaim it not merely to individuals in their personal and domestic lives. We do certainly have to do that. But we have to proclaim it as part of the continuing conversation which shapes public doctrine. It must be heard in the conversation of economists, psychiatrists, educators, scientists, and politicians. We have to proclaim it not as a package of estimable values, but as the truth about what is the case, about what every human being and every human society will have to reckon with. When we are faithful in this commission we are bound to appear subversive to those who believe that the cosmos is a closed system. We may appear to threaten the achievements of these centuries in which this has been the reigning belief. In truth we shall be offering the only hope of conserving and carrying forward the good fruits of these centuries into a future which might otherwise belong to the barbarians.

Speaking the Truth to Caesar

I recently reread a book which impressed me greatly when it first came out. Romano Guardini's *The End of the Modern World* was written immediately after the war amid the rubble of a ruined Germany. Guardini foresees the rapid erosion of the remnants of Christian culture which had survived and writes: "Christianity will once again need to prove itself deliberately as a faith which is not self-evident; it will be forced to distinguish itself more sharply from a dominant non-Christian ethos" (pp. 128-29). Although Europe has gone farther down the road which Guardini foresaw than America has, I think we can now all recognize this as a correct account of the situation in western and northern societies which once regarded themselves as the embodiment of Christian civilization. Guardini in the same passage says that the Church will have no alternative but to go back to its old dogmatic roots, and I have been trying to suggest how this might be done in a situation where the assumptions of our culture have driven a wedge through the Christian Church, dividing liberals from fundamentalists.

I want in this third chapter to look further into the question of what might be involved in the attempt to prove the validity and power of the Christian faith in the public life of a nation. During the long battle between these two parties in Christian society, those who label each other as liberals and fundamentalists, one of the main criticisms directed against the liberals was that they had substituted for the gospel of salvation through Jesus Christ a whole range of social and political issues, and that those who came to worship in their churches, hoping to hear the word of God spoken to their hearts and consciences, had to listen instead to a lecture on some social or political issue on which the preacher was less well informed than many of the listeners. On the other side, of course, the charge was made against fundamentalists and conservative evangelicals, that the gospel was being preached in a way that emptied it of its full ethical contents, that "cheap grace" was being peddled where there should have been a call to follow Jesus in challenging the wrongs of the world. I have to confess at once that there have been many occasions when I have felt betrayed in one or other of these ways, and I have a deep sympathy for the anger which this generated — on both sides of the dispute. Is it possible to say anything that could help the Church to avoid both of these betrayals and to bear a genuine gospel witness in face of the great public issues of society?

It is important to remember in the first place that there are situations in which the basic dogma in its starkest form is the most powerful critical agent in society. The celebration of the divine liturgy in churches of the USSR for the seventy years in which Marxism has ruled public life, and the faithful preaching of the word in Lutheran Churches for forty-five years in the German Democratic Republic, have been — as we now know — immensely powerful in creating a space in which the total claims of the state were quietly set aside in deference to one who is Lord of all states and kingdoms. That was, of course, the situation of the pre-Constantine Church of the first three centuries, the Church which was to carry civilization forward when the Roman world collapsed. We have had good reason in these past twelve months to realize again that the Church is an anvil that has worn out many hammers. But that is not our situation, and it is romantic nonsense to pretend that we could go back to a pre-Constantinian innocence. I say this because there are Christians who want to live in a state of perpetual protest, if not of persecution. There are Christians who seem to identify Christianity with protest against all forms of government because all government involves the use of coercion. But we live in a society where Christians, like others, have the responsibility of sharing in the business of government, even if it is only by casting a vote at fairly long intervals, and responsible citizenship entails much more than that.

And of course we cannot go back to that period of the Church's life which was inaugurated with the baptism of Constantine — that long period which created the civilization of Europe. Nostalgia for Christendom is very understandable but it is futile. We do indeed have to be grateful for those great centuries in which the barbarian tribes of the western peninsula of Asia were at least partially Christianized and the civilization was created of which we are the heirs and beneficiaries. To understand that period is essential if we are to understand ourselves. It was a sustained attempt to realize the reign of Christ in the actual life of the world. But it broke down, and we cannot try to reconstruct it.

The age which has followed it took its inspiration from the early achievements of the new science. It offered liberation from the dogma that had ruled Christendom and replaced it with the affirmation of the power of the individual human reason and conscience to discover, without the aid of divine revelation, what is the truth about the human situation. The central figure in public doctrine was no longer God, the creator and sustainer and guide of all things, but the individual human person who is equipped with the faculties necessary to know the truth and to live by it. It was perhaps almost inevitable that Christians, who do not live in a separate enclave but are part of society, should come to see the Church no longer as the bearer of the truth by which all human beings must live, but as a voluntary association in which individual believers might freely join themselves to develop and express their faith. These voluntary associations have obviously no intrinsic relation to the state. Church and state are not, as they were in the old Christendom, two organs of one body. Christianity is a matter of the relation of the individual soul to God, and the Church is there to help the individual to develop that relationship. In our own time we are seeing the later fruit of this in the fragmentation of Christian bodies and the multiplication of groups gathered around strong personalities who are able to appeal to the religious feelings of individuals.

There are, of course, certain advantages in this situation as compared with the situation of the Church in the Christendom period, when the power of the state could, and often did, force the Church into submission to worldly interests. It has been a particularly strong emphasis in the churches that stem from Calvin and the Geneva Reformation that the Church is not subject to the state in matters

spiritual. The freedom of the Church from domination by the state has been one of the key elements
in the Reformed tradition. But when this is combined, as it has been in modern liberal societies,
with the individualism to which the Enlightenment
gave birth; when the Church is seen simply as a
voluntary society made up of those individuals who
have decided to accept the Christian faith and to
join themselves together for its nourishment and
exercise, then the danger is that the ethical implications of the gospel come to be regarded as merely
house rules for the Church, guidance for Christian
behavior rather than the law of the creator with
jurisdiction over the entire human family. The freedom of the Church from control in spiritual matters
by the state is an empty freedom if it is simply the
freedom of individuals to follow their inclinations,
and not the freedom which is given by the word of
God to speak in the name of God to the state as to
every other human institution.

As we try to understand how the Church ought
to speak the word of God, the word of the gospel,
to the public life of our societies, I think that we
can be helped by looking at the most dramatic
confrontation in our time between the Church and
the public life of a nation, namely the German
church struggle. We may grant that the ideology
which took over the German nation in the 1930s
was a form of paganism much more extreme than

the one we have to face in our pluralist societies, but from an extreme case we can learn something for ourselves. It is well known that Dietrich Bonhoeffer, who was at the heart of that struggle and who had also been involved in church life in the USA and in Britain, had to face the fact that the good liberal Christians in the Anglo-Saxon world who supported the Confessing Church, supported it for reasons which that Church was bound to reject. As Bonhoeffer saw it, it was a question of the nature of the freedom of the Church. The Anglo-Saxon saw it as the absence of limitation: the Church was not controlled by the state. To Bonhoeffer and his colleagues that was no freedom at all. The freedom of the Church is that which it has when it is obedient to the word of God, the freedom which the Church has even when its preachers are put in prison. The supreme testimony to this freedom in that context was the Barmen Declaration. This does not talk about freedom but about obedience, about the fact that the Church has to obey the Lord Jesus Christ and no other power. The Barmen text did not discuss political or economic issues which are the proper business of politicians and economists. But it was an incomparably powerful and effective assertion of the freedom which the word of God gives to the Church. For the Church simply to be free to do its own thing is not freedom. The proper freedom of the Church is inseparable from its obligation to declare the sovereignty of Christ over every sphere of human life without exception. The individualistic model of freedom which pervades our society and controls the way we approach every question has to be challenged by the gospel affirmation that we are not naturally free but that we may receive the gift of freedom when we are in Christ, and that in every area of life there is only one Lord to be obeyed, namely the Lord Jesus Christ.

How is this to be worked out in the life of the Church and in its preaching? I think there are two issues which have to be distinguished as we ask this question; one is about the relation between law and gospel, the other about the relation between personal behavior and public policy. The first is such a well-worn issue that I hesitate to refer to it, but it is one of the main charges against the liberal brand of preachers that they do not preach the gospel but advocate political programs. Peter Berger in his charge of apostasy against the American churches seems to adopt a view of the gospel which reduces it entirely to the forgiveness of sins. But the precious gift of forgiveness can never be separated from the call of Jesus to take up the cross and follow. It is the very heart of the gospel that it both gives everything and requires everything. The task of the preacher is to hold these together so that men and women are both released from the burden of guilt and also set free to follow Jesus. It is true that a great deal of preaching on political issues has the effect of laying a still heavier burden of guilt on those who are not tough-minded enough to shrug it all off. People, and especially good conscientious people who are aware of the terrible evil in the world, do need the message of forgiveness. They cannot effectively address the evils of the world while they are crushed by the load of guilt. The guilt feeling of the white liberal is an important part of the present scene. But it is a distorted preaching of the gospel which does not lead to fresh commitment to follow Jesus in challenging the domination of evil.

That is all easily said but hard to do, as every preacher knows. But I go on to the more complex question about the ethical content of preaching. Few Christians would deny that there are necessary ethical commitments in being a Christian. To love the neighbor is the necessary implication of following Jesus. But what does love entail? Does it entail commitment to specific political, economic, and social programs? Is such commitment an improper encroachment of the Church into the sphere of government? Or is the absence of such commitment an evasion of the challenge of the gospel?

There is certainly a long and rather sad history of alliances between the Church and particular political programs. The Church has been committed to the defense of the divine right of kings, of oligarchy against democracy and of free market capitalism against communism. In Britain the Free Churches were so comprehensively committed to the liberal party that when the latter collapsed they went into a decline from which they have not recovered. The Church cannot be totally identified with any of these causes. And yet it cannot be indifferent to them. Perhaps the most important thing to say, and it is important even if it is negative, is this. The affirmations of the Barmen Declaration would have made no impact without the anathemas. The Declaration names and rejects a false ideology. It does not tell the German people what to do in the area of politics. It affirms the truth of the gospel and, in its light, condemns the reigning falsehood. I think that perhaps that is the first thing to say about the duty of the Church in relation to political issues. The Church has to unmask ideologies.

Walter Wink in his series of volumes on the principalities and powers has helped us to see afresh the relevance to our situation of the biblical language about the powers. It is not true, Wink reminds us, that the Church's message is addressed only to individual people. It is, according to Ephesians 3:10, to be made known to the principalities and powers. We meet these powers, as the New Testament tells us, in such entities as the state, the law, tradition, and religion. These powers, although ordained by God, because they did not know the true wisdom of God, combined to crucify the Lord of glory. But while we meet them in these forms, they have a reality which is not exhausted by these visible representatives, Caiaphas and Pilate and Herod, so that our wrestling is not with these men of flesh and blood, but with the powers which are represented in them. And these powers, while created in Christ and for Christ, having therefore a positive function in God's economy, can be and have been corrupted. They are corrupted, become demonic, when they are absolutized, given the place which belongs only to God. The good gift of kinship in the narrower and wider family is corrupted into the evil of racism. And the good gift of individual personality is corrupted into the evil ideology of individualism.

The ideology which the Barmen Declaration sought to unmask and to reject was the ideology of nation and race and blood. The ideology which we have to recognize, unmask, and reject is an ideology of freedom, a false and idolatrous conception of freedom which equates it with the freedom of each individual to do as he or she wishes. We have to set against it the Trinitarian faith which sees all reality in terms of relatedness. In explicit rejection of an individualism which puts the autonomous self at the center and sees other selves as limitations on our freedom, we have to set the basic dogma entrusted to us, namely that freedom is to be found by being taken into that community of love given and received which is the eternal reality from which and for which all things exist. The rejection of relatedness as the true road to freedom is seen in the easy dissolution of the marriage bond, in the breakup of families, and in the massive development of consumerism.

Its most formidable manifestation is the contemporary ideology of the free market. Here again we have an example of something good being corrupted. It is clear, and the lesson has been driven home in the past twelve months, that free markets are the best way of continuously balancing supply and demand. But it is also clear that when the free market is made into an absolute, outside of rational control in the light of ethical principles, it becomes a power that enslaves human beings. The free market is a good servant but a bad master. It is not necessary to argue the point that, if we take the human family as a whole, what is experienced as freedom by a minority is experienced as bondage by a majority. Adam Smith himself recognized that free markets would only work for the common good if certain moral principles permeated society. His successors have detached economics altogether from ethics and made it an autonomous science. For purposes of such a science, human beings are supposed to be motivated only by self-interest. The basic unit of society is a human being who, with single-minded purpose, seeks to acquire the maximum of goods and services with the minimum of effort. At an early stage in the evolution of free-market capitalism it became obvious that it was producing the abominations of child labor and the destruction of human health and dignity. In a moral revulsion against these things, developed nations introduced the legislation which limited the operations of the market and created what we have known as the welfare state. Much of this legislation is being dismantled in some of the developed societies, but the ecological threat now confronts us with new evidence that the free market cannot be left uncontrolled. The idea that if economic life is detached from all moral considerations and left to operate by its own laws all will be well is simply an abdication of human responsibility. It is the handing over of human life to the pagan goddess of fortune. If Christ's sovereignty is not recognized in the world of economics, then demonic powers take control.

It is not the business of the Church to make an alliance with either the right or the left in the present political scene. It has to unmask the ideologies that permeate them and offer a more rational model for the understanding of the human situation. Both sides in the argument use the language of the rights of the individual. On the one side there is the right of every individual to do what he wants with what he has lawfully earned. On the other side there is the right of every individual to have her needs met. The argument is irresolvable on rational grounds for two reasons. First, in a society which has no accepted public doctrine about the purpose for which all things and all persons exist, there is no basis for adjudicating between needs and wants. A rational person would *want* exactly what he or she *needs* to fulfill the purpose for which we exist. In the absence of a public doctrine about that purpose, the dispute between wants and needs is irresolvable. Secondly, both parties rely on the concept of the rights of the individual. These rights are part of public doctrine enshrined in legislation. But rights are totally void of meaning unless there are parties who acknowledge the responsibility to meet the claim of right. Since there is no corresponding public doctrine about human responsibility, the multiple and contrary claims to right can only destroy society.

The language of "rights" is, of course, a product of the Enlightenment. The older Christian society spoke about duties which were owed to God and to the neighbor. In the language of the Enlightenment, when rights are violated we speak about justice; in the earlier language one talked about sin and punishment. The sin is against God, and the punishment is his work, in whom punishment is only the dark side of mercy. The Church, in its general domestication into the culture of the Enlightenment, has adopted the same language; it speaks much of rights and of justice, little of sin and punishment. If there is no judge, then justice is as each of us defines it and rival claims for right are mere conflicts of interest which rend the fabric of society to shreds. We have the responsibility to bear witness that there is a judge of all the nations, that his judgment is replete with mercy, and that the clue to all public issues as to all personal life is to be found at the one mercy seat where the sin of the whole human race was both judged and pardoned.

If, then, the Church is not to identify itself with any particular political program, and yet cannot leave political issues out of her concern, as though the sovereignty of Christ did not extend beyond the walls of the Church, what can be said by way of guidance in this area? I come back to the Barmen Declaration as a model. Each of its clauses has an affirmation and an anathema. The first duty is affirmation. The Church must affirm the truth of the gospel, the fact of the sovereignty of Christ as sole Lord and Savior, and the Trinitarian faith, the given starting point, the dogma which must shape all our thinking and revising. To affirm this in season and out of season, whether they hear or refuse to hear, is in fact the most radical political action that we can take. Behind the rather violent charge of apostasy made by Peter Berger and his colleagues there is this element of validity. It *is* the case that many Christians have a rather tepid faith in this fundamental dogma and therefore tend to invest the zeal and the commitment which are properly owed to it in particular moral and political causes. We get the widespread phenomenon of single-issue Christians, Christians for whom the whole of Christianity is equated with support for a particular cause and the Church is valued only as it supports that cause. Moral and political commitments which are legitimate implications of the Christian faith in a particular situation are allowed to displace the fundamental dogma. And it follows, of course, that those who regard other issues as the urgent ones for here and now are effectively excommunicated. Once again, that which is good and proper at its own level is corrupted when it is absolutized.

Therefore, with affirmation there has to be anathema. We have to reject ideologies which give to particular elements in God's ordering of things the central and absolute place which belongs to Christ alone. It is good to love and serve the nation in which God has set us; we need more, not less true patriotism. But to give absolute commitment to the nation is to go into bondage. Family and kinship are precious gifts to be loved and cherished, but racism is a corruption of what is good. The mutuality of man and woman in God's image is among the most precious of God's gifts, and feminism may be a legitimate protest against the evils of male dominance, but if it becomes the focus of ultimate commitment it becomes idolatrous. The free market is a good way of balancing supply and demand. If it is absolutized and allowed to rule economic life, it becomes an evil power.

If the Church is clear and bold in its affirmation of the truth of the gospel as the reality by which all human enterprises are to be tested and in its unmasking and rejecting of the idols whose worshippers fill so much of the not-so-naked public square, then there is room for a great deal of pragmatism, of experiment, of venturing in relation to specific issues. This implies that different Christians will commit themselves to different causes but will not excommunicate one another for so doing. But to say this is not enough. I would like to make three further points which I hope are helpful.

First, while the Church as a corporate society cannot identify itself with particular political programs, it must be the responsibility of the Church to equip its members for active and informed participation in public life in such a way that the Christian faith shapes that participation. Public life is the area where the principalities and powers operate. There are structures and forces which have a transpersonal character. The person who operates within them is not free to act as if he or she was a free individual. There is some freedom, but it is limited by the structure as a whole. If I understand the teaching of the New Testament on this matter, I understand the role of the Christian as that of being neither a conservative nor an anarchist, but a subversive agent. When Paul says that Christ has disarmed the powers (not destroyed them), and when he speaks of the powers as being created in Christ and for Christ, and when he says that the Church is to make known the wisdom of God to the powers, I take it that this means that a Christian neither accepts them as some sort of eternal order which cannot be changed, nor seeks to destroy them because of the evil they do, but seeks to subvert them from within and thereby to bring them back under the allegiance of their true Lord.

There is a beautiful illustration of this in Paul's dealing with the runaway slave Onesimus. In the letter which goes to Colossae he tells Christian slaves to obey their earthly masters, because they are in fact serving the Lord in doing so. He does not tell Onesimus to go underground in Rome or wherever. He sends him back to his master as a slave, but he sends him back with the status of an apostolic nuncio. The structure is not to be simply smashed — as so much popular political rhetoric advocates; it is to be subverted from within.

But undercover agents need a great deal of skill. We do not spend enough of our energies in training undercover agents. A psychiatrist who was a devout Christian was recently asked whether her Christianity informed her work in the consulting room. She replied: "But that would be unprofessional conduct." What kind of preparation is needed to enable a psychiatrist to discern the ways in which her profession could be subverted from its allegiance to other principles and become an area where the saving work of Christ is acknowledged? What would be the specific kind of training for a teacher in the public schools, for an executive in a big corporation, for a lawyer or a civil servant? Do we not need to invest much more of the Church's resources in creating the possibility for such training. It cannot be done by clergy, though they have a part. It calls for the vigorous development of lay programs in which those in specific areas of secular work can explore together the possibilities of subversion. I know that much has been said along these lines, and yet there is little to show for it. In small enterprises of this kind in which I have been involved I have found that there was great enthusiasm once the purpose was understood. For undercover agents, it is a great thing to know that you are not alone.

If I may move from the rather shady metaphor of the undercover agent to a more respectable one, is not this what is meant in the great passage of the first letter of Peter where he speaks of the Church as a holy priesthood? The priest has to represent God to us and to represent us to God. The Church, says Peter, is to do those two things: to show forth to the world the mighty acts of God, and to offer to God the spiritual sacrifices due to him. This priesthood is, clearly, something to be exercised in the midst of the secular life of the world. Every Christian in the course of secular employment is to be present as representative of the whole priesthood, thus bringing the secular world into its proper relation to God. The Church gathers on the Lord's Day to renew the priesthood by renewing its incorporation in the one High Priest. It should become part of the normal work of the Church to equip its members for the exercise of this priesthood in the many different areas of secular life, and in terms of the specific powers that rule in these areas.

Second, if such training were widely available, we could look for a time when many of those holding responsible positions of leadership in public life were committed Christians equipped to raise the questions and make the innovations in these areas which the gospel requires. Whenever the question is raised about the duty of the Church to reclaim public life for the Christian faith, the specter of a return to theocracy, to a reconstructed Christendom, is raised. But I cannot accept the view

that there is no third way between a purely priva-
tized Christianity and a Muslim style theocracy. If
we accept the model of what I have called a committed pluralism, we can look for and work for a
time when Christian leadership (not Christian domination) can shape society, shape the plausibility
structure within which people make their decisions
and come to their beliefs. I know that by using the
word "leadership" I am laying myself open to the
charge of elitism, that most unforgivable among the
current list of unforgivable sins. I decline to be
intimidated. Elitism has become a bad word because
we have had too much experience of self-serving
elites. But the remedy is not to deny the necessity
for leadership; that is simply evasion. It is the summons to a leadership which is modeled on that of
the one whose words "Follow me" are constitutive
of the Church.

Third, the most important contribution which
the Church can make to a new social order is to be
itself a new social order. More fundamental than
any of the things which the Church can say or do
is the reality of a new society which allows itself to
be shaped by the Christian faith. The basic unit of
that new society is the local congregation. I have
the impression that the local congregation has too
often been regarded in the best ecumenical circles
as something which needs to be dragged along
rather than as the primal engine of change in society.

Our powerful denominational and interdenominational agencies for social and political action develop ways of thinking and speaking which distances them from the ordinary congregation. This, I think, is one of the reasons why we get snared in the problem of law and gospel. Our political and social programs are detached from the gospel of forgiveness which is, or should be, announced in Church. Our programs are not recognizable as the natural expression of what we do and say and hear on Sunday morning in Church. They become simply programs alongside of, or meshed with, the programs of political parties and secular pressure groups.

I realize that this is to some extent unavoidable, because the evils we have to address are on a large scale and need to be addressed at the national and international level. The local community cannot address them alone. But the local Christian congregation, where the word of the gospel is preached, where in the sacrament of the Eucharist we are united with Christ in his dying for the sin of the world and in his risen life for the sake of the world, is the place where we are enabled to develop a shared life in which sin can be both recognized and forgiven. If this congregation understands its true character as a holy priesthood for the sake of the world, and if its members are equipped for the exercise of that priesthood in their secular employments, then there is a point of growth for a new social order. Even if it is a very small congregation, and perhaps even especially when it is a small congregation, it can thus become the growing point from which the subversion of the principalities and powers and the first shoots of a new creation can develop. This is in no way a substitute for the kind of political actions that are needed on the national and international scale. But it is the necessary groundwork without which political action on the macroscale will always fail.

I want to affirm the fundamental importance of the local congregation. There is much that the Church needs which is on a wider scale, both to help and encourage the local congregation and to address the larger units of society such as the city, the state, or the nation. But there is a sense in which the local congregation is the place where the truth of the gospel is tested and experienced in the most basic way. But it must be a place where the gospel is preached and believed. I have spent a good deal of time discussing the way in which our preaching of the gospel has been confused and muffled by the quarrel between liberals and fundamentalists. I believe that this is an unnecessary quarrel arising from the fact that both sides have been seduced by the unquestioned assumptions of our culture. We shall prove our faithfulness to the gospel by being both fundamentalist and liberal: fundamentalist in the sense that we acknowledge no other foundation upon which to build either our thinking or our acting, either our private or our public life, than the Lord Jesus Christ as he is known to us through the Scriptures; and liberal in the sense that we are ready to live in a plural society, open to new experience, ready to listen to new ideas, always pressing forward toward fuller understanding in the confidence that Jesus is indeed the true and living way, and that when we follow him we are not lost.

This emphasis on the local Church will be misunderstood and misapplied if we do not remember that the local congregation is the local presence of the one holy catholic and apostolic Church that we acknowledge in the creeds. The local congregation is not a branch of the universal Church, but it is the place where the universal Church is made visible. When the local congregation speaks and acts, its words and acts must claim to be the words and acts of the universal Church if they are to be authentic. But this is hard to achieve, or even to acknowledge, in our divided state. In the past three hundred years, mainly because of events in European history, churches have come to see themselves more as national churches than as the visible presence of the universal Church. With the breakup of the old Christendom, the national state became the one recognized center of sovereignty. Churches have been seduced into thinking of themselves as the church *of* the nation, rather than as the church *for* the nation, the church that can speak a word of God *to* the nation. But, to speak of purely secular realities, we may well be coming to the end of the era of the sovereign nation-state as we have known it for the past three centuries. Economic, financial, and technical forces have created a global system that is far more powerful than most existing states. The secular powers shaping human life are increasingly transnational. If the Church is to speak the truth to Caesar, it is these powers that must be more and more in our sights.

Experience in the ecumenical movement has taught many of us how very hard it is for national churches to accept words of warning and correction from the wider Christian community. The World Council of Churches, which is not the universal Church but a council of divided churches seeking unity, has provided many of us with a taste of this experience. It can be painful; it is often rejected; but it is necessary. The local congregation is not true to its calling if it allows itself to forget that its only title deeds are as the local presence of the catholic Church. Having myself had the privilege of sharing in many assemblies of the World Council, I have found it a salutary exercise in the course of sermon preparation to imagine myself preaching that sermon in a WCC assembly, and to ask myself, "Would it ring true *there*?" If one evades this kind of question, then the congregation may be a warm religious fellowship but it will not be the catholic Church locally embodied.

These thoughts lead into areas beyond the scope of these chapters. If the local congregation is to be true to its calling, if it is to be able to speak the truth to Caesar's local representatives, then it must seek such ordering of its life that all it is and does is true to its catholic character. Its ministry must be acknowledged as the ministry of the whole Church, its baptism as baptism into the universal Church, its eucharistic celebration a celebration of the one universal family.

And this leads us into the issues of faith and order that were so fundamental in the early work of the ecumenical movement but that are now so sadly marginalized. If it is true, as I have said, that the chief contribution of the Church to the renewing of social order is to be itself a new social order, then these issues are central. In a world that is now knit together into a single global city, the Church must be visible and recognizable as the community that embraces the whole city in the Father's love. The word of truth that the Church speaks to Caesar must be, or must aim to be, the word of the whole Church. Splintered, confused, and compromised, the Church seldom sounds worth listening to. But the Church has outlasted many occupants of Caesar's throne and will outlast many more, for the truth entrusted to her is the truth of God.